How do I feel about

OUR NEW BABY

Jen Green

Franklin Watts London • Sydney

An Aladdin Book
© Aladdin Books Ltd 1997

Designed and produced by
Aladdin Books Ltd
28 Percy Street
London
W1P 0LD

First published in Great Britain
in 1997 by Franklin Watts
96 Leonard Street
London
EC2A 4RH

ISBN: 0 7496 2818 9 (hb)
ISBN: 0 7496 3630 0 (pb)

A catalogue record for this book
is available from the British Library.

Printed in Belgium
Designer   Gary Edgar-Hyde
Editor   Sarah Levete
Illustrator   Christopher
                O'Neill
Photographer   Roger Vlitos

The author, Jen Green, has
written extensively for children.

Contents

Introduction 3

Expecting A Baby 4

Mixed Feelings 6

The Birth 10

A Newborn Baby 14

My New Brother Or Sister . 18

Don't Forget 22

Index 24

Introduction

Dean, Rosie, Max and May are in the same class at school. Dean's mum is expecting a new baby and so is Rosie's mum. New babies bring changes to any family. Dean, May, Max and Rosie talk about what a new brother or sister will mean to them.

To begin with, I was unsure about the new baby.

I have a great time with my brother and sister.

MAX

ROSIE

At first it may feel strange with a new baby at home.

New babies are a lot of fun!

MAY

DEAN

Expecting A Baby

Dean and Max are good friends at school. Dean has been looking forward to telling Max his news. Dean's mum is pregnant – she will be having a new baby. The baby will be born in five months' time. Dean is excited about having a new baby brother or sister to play with. Is a new baby expected in your family?

You can have fun in a small family...

... or in a large family.

▼ Where Do Babies Come From?

All babies begin from a tiny egg and a seed, called a sperm. The egg comes from the mother. The sperm comes from the father. When they join together, a new baby begins inside the mother.

◄ How Babies Grow

A baby grows in the mother's womb, near the stomach. At first the new baby is tiny, but slowly it gets bigger. The mother's tummy gets larger, too. If your mum is pregnant you may be able to feel the baby moving in her tummy.

Dean, how do you feel about the new baby?

"I'm really excited. I've already got a younger sister, Sonia. I was only three when she was born so I don't remember much about it. This time I'm going to the clinic with mum for her check-up. There's a special machine there which shows you the shape of the baby on a TV screen."

Mixed Feelings

Rosie lives with her mum and her stepdad, Steve. When Rosie went home with the news about Dean's family, Rosie's mum told her that she was also expecting a baby. Rosie says she has mixed feelings about it. Dean says that his little sister Sonia is also unhappy about the news. If a new baby is expected in your family, how do you feel about it?

You may feel happy …

…or you may feel unhappy.

▼ Stepfamilies

If you live with only one of your parents, and your mum or dad is expecting a baby with a new partner, you might feel a bit left out. You might feel the new baby will get more love. But a new baby won't change your mum or dad's love for you. There will be enough love to go round for everyone.

Sorry, I'm too tired to play.

Why don't they want to see my picture?

◄ Pleased or Cross?

When a baby is expected, you may feel excited or proud. But you may also feel bored or impatient if your mum is feeling tired. You might also feel cross if she can't play with you as much as she did before.

▶ How Your Mum Feels

If your mum is expecting a baby, she may feel sick in the mornings. She may need more rest than usual. This is nothing to worry about. A growing baby uses up lots of your mum's energy. As the baby gets bigger, your mum may need help to lift heavy things.

7

Mixed Feelings

1. A new baby was due in Hari's family. Hari was worried about it.

2. Hari's dad realised Hari was upset. He asked him what was wrong.

3. Hari's dad said that Hari had an important part to play in the family.

Why was Hari feeling worried?

If a new baby is due in your family, it's natural to feel a bit anxious. Like Hari, you may feel pleased, but also wonder quite how things will be. Hari talked to his dad. His dad explained they were so happy with Hari that they decided to have a new baby, too.

If you feel worried, talk to your parents. Your mum and dad will understand how you feel.

▼ Getting Ready

There are many things to prepare for a new baby. The baby will need somewhere to sleep. You may have to move your things around, or move to a new room. Do you have any old toys which the new baby may like to play with?

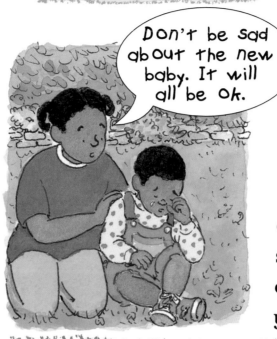

Don't be sad about the new baby. It will all be Ok.

◄ All Change

A baby means change for everyone. You may find this easy or you may find it hard, and wish that things could stay the way they were. If you already have a little brother or sister, he or she might feel upset about no longer being the youngest child.

Are you looking forward to the new baby, Rosie?

"Yes and no. My mum and dad don't live together any more. Now mum and my stepdad, Steve, are having a new baby. I thought the new baby might be more special to them than me. But mum says that having a new baby won't change the way she feels about me."

The Birth

It's May's birthday today. Max is giving May a card and present to celebrate. May is now eight years old. Eight years ago today she was born in hospital. May says she was born at nine o' clock in the morning. Do you know what happened when you were born? Where did it happen and who was there?

It's often a rush before the birth.

A birthday is a very special day.

▼ *In Hospital*

After nine months in the mother's womb, the new baby is ready to be born. Your mum may go into hospital to have her baby. Your dad may go with her. While the baby is being born, your parents will ask a relative or a close friend to come and look after you.

◄ *At Home*

Your mum may decide to have her baby at home. A midwife, who is a special person who helps to deliver a baby, may come to help your mum. Your mum and dad may also arrange for a relative or friend to take care of you for a short while.

▶ *How Long?*

A baby's birth may take only a few hours. Or it can take most of a day. If your mum goes to hospital to have her baby, she may be home a few hours after it is born. Or she may stay in hospital for a few days. It's a big day when the baby comes home at last.

1. Fred's mum was having a baby in hospital. Fred's dad rang to speak to him.

2. The next day Fred went to see his mum in hospital. Fred's mum gave him a special hug.

3. Fred was excited when he saw the baby. His mum let Fred hold him for a while.

How did Fred feel about the birth of his baby brother?

Fred missed his mum when she was in hospital, even though his favourite aunt looked after him. When his dad rang to tell him about his new brother, Fred wasn't sure what he felt. But when he saw his mum, everything felt fine again. Don't worry if your mum goes away to have her baby. She and your dad will soon be home.

▽ Ready to Play?

You may want to play with your new brother or sister straight away. But new-born babies don't play much at first. They mostly sleep and feed. But they do like to be cuddled. Support the baby's head while you are cuddling him or her.

◁ Growing Up

Things change fast with a new baby. After three months the baby will be awake for longer, and will want you to play with him or her. Soon the baby will eat solid food. You might like to help with feeding – it may be messy!

May, do you know what happened when you were born?

"Yes, my mum told me. I was born in hospital. Mum said it took sixteen hours for me to be born. She said she was very pleased when I arrived at last! I've got two younger sisters. They were both born at home. My youngest sister, Jo, only took four hours to be born."

A Newborn Baby

Max's teacher asked everyone in the class to bring in photos of themselves as babies. They stuck the photos on the wall and guessed who was who. No-one guessed which one was Max. Later Max and Rosie talked about babies. Do you know what you were like as a baby? Did you cry or sleep a lot?

Newborn babies are so small. I'd be scared to hold one.

Mum says you must hold them firmly but carefully.

A baby feeds from the mum's breast.

Or a baby feeds from a bottle.

▼ Playing With The Baby

Newborn babies are very small at first – but don't be scared to play with them! Babies like to look at people's faces. They learn to talk by copying the sounds we make so sing nursery rhymes and talk to the baby.

Make the baby laugh by being as silly as you like!

◀ Why Do Babies Cry?

Crying is a baby's only way of saying he or she needs something. A baby cries to get attention, if they are hungry or uncomfortable, or bored.

Don't feel upset if the baby cries. You may get really good at knowing what the baby wants.

▶ Sleeping Problems

New babies need to feed often, including at night. Your mum and dad will be tired if they get up several times at night.

You may also sleep badly, especially if you can hear the baby crying. There is nothing to worry about, so try to relax at night.

15

1. Ayisha and her family were very excited. The new baby had just come home.

2. But when friends came round, the baby was the centre of attention. Ayisha felt left out.

3. Later Ayisha talked it over with her mum.

Why was Ayisha upset?

Ayisha was really pleased about the new baby. But she got upset when she felt no-one was taking any notice of her any more. Things may feel different at first with a new baby at home. It will take time to get used to having a little stranger in the family. Talk things over with your mum and dad. Talking about your feelings nearly always helps.

▽ Good Times

You will probably have lots of different feelings about the baby. You may feel really pleased most of the time. You may love to play with the baby, and enjoy bath-times or feeds. You may be best at making the baby laugh.

◁ Fed Up?

Sometimes you may feel bored or fed up about the baby. You may feel your mum and dad now have less time for you. Talk to your parents. Perhaps you can agree on a special time for you and your mum or dad.

Max, what was it like in your family when you were little?

"My older brother was eight and my sister was four when I was born. Mum said they helped a lot when I was little. They played with me and helped teach me to talk and to read. I learnt to walk quickly so I could keep up with them!"

My New Brother Or Sister

May and Dean are showing each other pictures of the people in their families, which they drew at school. Dean said he and his sister, Sonia, play together a lot. May said she used to get on badly with her younger sister, Amy, but now they are good friends. If you've got brothers and sisters, how do you get on with them?

My sister Sonia is really good at making up games.

I get a bit cross when Amy beats me at cards.

Some brothers and sisters get on.

Others seem to fight a lot.

▽ *Talking, Walking*

Of course, you can do hundreds of things a baby cannot do. Young babies cannot feed themselves or use a potty. But they grow up fast. At six months, a baby may start to crawl. At nine months, he or she may begin to say a few words.

▷ *Younger Brothers And Sisters*

If you have a younger brother or sister, he or she may not feel as you do about the baby. He or she is more likely to feel angry and a bit left out.

  If you spend time with your little brother or sister, it can really help them to feel special, too.

◁ *Safety First*

Babies have no idea about what is safe. They put things into their mouths to taste them and to see if they are soft or hard. But you know what is not safe to eat, and places that aren't safe to go near. This can really help when you are keeping an eye on the baby.

1. Jack felt that his mum only ever played with his new sister. He felt angry and hit his mum.

2. Jack said his mum didn't care about him. Jack's mum said hitting wasn't allowed.

3. Next time he felt angry, Jack kicked a football. After a while he felt a bit better.

Why did Jack feel angry?

With the new baby, Jack felt cross and left out. Like him, you might feel angry. After all, you didn't choose to have a new baby in your family. You may feel like breaking something or even hitting someone. But this would only make things worse. Talk about your feelings. If you still feel like hitting out, hit something soft, like a cushion, or kick a football outside.

▽ Family Fights

Sometimes you may quarrel with your brother or sister. But you probably stick up for each other when it matters most. Some brothers and sisters quarrel a lot when they are young, but become good friends later.

◁ Sharing

You may feel jealous of your brother or sister. You may find it hard to share your mum and dad.

But just because your parents love your new sister or brother, doesn't mean they will love you any less.

How do you get on with your sisters, May?

"Amy was born when I was three. I felt a bit jealous of her at first. Then, when I was six and Amy was three, Jo was born. I liked playing with Jo, but I could see Amy felt angry. I told Amy I knew how she was feeling. Now Amy and I play together lots."

21

Don't Forget . . .

How do you feel now about the new baby in your family, Rosie?

"At first I didn't like the idea of lots of change. After mum and I talked about it, I felt better. I talked things over with Steve, my stepdad. I'm looking forward to it now. I'm going to help choose the baby's name."

Does a new baby make a big difference to a family, Dean?

"You may feel as if you get your own way less when there is a new baby around. But no-one gets their own way all the time. Having a new baby in our family helped me to see that other people's feelings were important too. It's good, too, because we can have lots of fun now that our family is bigger."

22

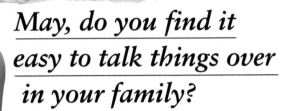

May, do you find it easy to talk things over in your family?

"When my sister Amy was small, for a bit I thought that mum and dad loved her more than me. But I told mum and dad how I felt.

They said that they loved us both just as much, but sometimes Amy needed more looking after because she was a baby."

Do you like having a brother and sister, Max?

"Yeah. It's great. I learned from my big brother and sister. There's a video of my brother teaching me to walk. It's really funny. Now that I'm older, we all have even more fun together."

Index

C c

Changes 3, 7, 9, 22

Crying 15

F f

Feeling angry 7, 19, 20, 21

Feeling excited 5, 7, 12

Feeling fed up 6, 7, 17

Feeling happy 6

Feeing jealous 21

Feeling left out 16

Feeling unhappy 6

Feeling worried 8

G g Getting ready 9

H h

Having a baby at home 11, 12

Having a baby in hospital 11, 12

Having fun with brothers and sisters 4, 18, 23

How a baby grows 5, 7, 13, 19

L l Looking after a new baby 19, 23

P p Playing 13, 15, 17

Q q Quarrels 18, 21

S s Stepfamilies 7, 9, 22

T t Talking about feelings 8, 16, 17, 23

All the photographs in this book have been posed by models. The publishers would like to thank them all.